KEEPSAKES

for the Heart

KEEPSAKES
for the Heart

FRIENDSHIP

Compiled by Alice Gray

Multnomah® Publishers—Sisters, Oregon

PRESENTED
to

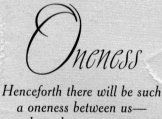

Oneness

Henceforth there will be such
a oneness between us—
that when one weeps
the other will taste salt.

—Author unknown

CONTENTS

The Crazy Quilt

I have an old quilt made by my father's grandmother. It's not a beautiful quilt, and all the fabric appears to be quite old. But I love it.

The pieces are probably leftover scraps from Aunt Fran's apron, little Mary's Easter dress, or Grampa's favorite shirt. They are odd shapes and sizes. Some nameless shapes have hooks and curves, long slivers of fabric painstakingly sewn with dozens of meticulous stitches. A few tiny patches are smaller than my thumbnail.

Some of the fabric is very plain with dull color. I can just hear some tired mother say, "But, dear, it's a very serviceable cloth...," while her daughter frowns at the new school dress. Other pieces are bright and cheery, like snippets of birthdays, summer vacations, and fun times gone by. A few fancier pieces are satiny smooth with embossing or embroidery; they seem to whisper of weddings, dances, a first kiss....

My father's grandmother was nearly blind and perhaps that explains why the shades appear haphazardly arranged and almost seem to shout at each other. I wonder if she ever realized what her creations looked like, or did she simply go by touch? They do have an interesting texture—smooth next to bumpy, seersucker alongside velvet; and all over the quilt hundreds of tiny stitches, almost invisible to the eye, pucker ever so slightly.

If I were blind, I would like to make quilts like this.

Recently my own family relocated to a new town, and I was in bed with the flu, wrapped in my great grandmother's crazy quilt. I felt sorry for myself and I missed the friends I'd left behind. Deep down, I knew it was partly my own fault—I hadn't taken steps to establish new friendships. Several acquaintances seemed willing, but I was holding back, hesitating....

As I studied the crazy quilt, I thought of the many friends I'd had throughout my life. Some felt a bit scratchy and rough like a sturdy piece of wool, but in time they softened—or I became used to them. Others were delicate like silk and needed to be handled with care. Some were colorful and bright and great fun to be with. A few special others felt soft and cozy like flannel, and they knew how to make me feel better.

Many of my friends have only been around for a season. So often I've had to leave them behind, or they leave me! And yet, in my heart, I know they are friends for life. If I met them on the street tomorrow, we would hug and laugh and talk nonstop. It would seem like yesterday.

And that's because God has sewn them into my heart.

I pulled the old quilt closer around me, comforted and warmed by my memories. Surely, my own master-piece—this quilt of friendships I fretted over—was not nearly finished, I would make new friends in this town. And like my great grandmother, trusting her fingers to lead her, I would, by faith, reach out.

—*Melody Carlson*
from Patchwork of Love

Chance Meeting

They shared a neighborhood and street, these friends, shared good memories, good times. When each wife became a widow within weeks of the other, they shared in mourning, too. The women made a pact that no hour would be too late to wake the other when the memories and loss became so great that only a friend's embrace could get them through. No need to call ahead, just knock on the other's door. Each agreed to give in this special way.

One night the grief became so great it woke her, the anguish so real it sliced through her troubled sleep. In her night dress, she fled into the darkness seeking solace at her neighbor's door. She did not make it. Instead, she met her friend mid-street, equally seeking, reaching for the comfort found only inside understanding arms.

—Jane Kirkpatrick
from A Burden Shared

Summer and Winter

I remember as a little girl I would sometimes run home from school with big news to share with my grandmother.

"Oh Nanna! I have met the most wonderful little girl! We're going to be real pals. She just moved here and she's in my class, and oh, she's tremendous! We're going to be best friends."

My grandmother would say to me, "Dear, you have to summer with her and winter with her, and summer with her again. Then tell me."

—*Pamela Reeve*
from Relationships

At the Winter Feeder

His feather flame doused dull
by ice and cold,
the cardinal hunched
into the rough, green feeder
but ate no seed.

Through binoculars I saw
festered and useless
his beak, broken
at the root.

Then two: one blazing, one gray,
rode the swirling weather
into my vision
and lighted at his side.

Unhurried, as if possessing
the patience of God,
they cracked sunflowers
and fed him
beak to wounded beak
choice meats.

Each morning and afternoon
the winter long,
that odd triumvirate,
that trinity of need,
returned and ate
their sacrament
of broken seed.

—John Leax
from The Task of Adam

Beethoven's Gift

A story is told about Beethoven, a man not known for social grace. Because of his deafness, he found conversation difficult and humiliating. When he heard of the death of a friend's son, Beethoven hurried to the house, overcome with grief. He had no words of comfort to offer. But he saw a piano in the room. For the next half hour he played the piano, pouring out his emotions in the most eloquent way he could. When he finished playing, he left. The friend later remarked that no one else's visit had meant so much.

— *Philip Yancey*
from Helping the Hurting

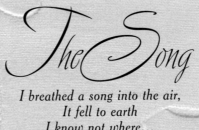

The Song

I breathed a song into the air,
It fell to earth
I know not where...
And the song,
from beginning to end,
I found again
In the heart of a friend.

—Henry Wadsworth
Longfellow

Teardrops of Hope

My friend Lauri and I had brought out our kids to the park that day to celebrate my 35th birthday. From a picnic table we watched them laugh and leap through the playground while we unpacked a basket bulging with sandwiches and cookies.

We toasted our friendship with bottles of mineral water. It was then that I noted Lauri's new drop earrings. In the 13 years I'd known Lauri, she'd always loved drop earrings. I'd seen her wear pair after pair: threaded crystals cast in blue, strands of colored gemstones, beaded pearls in pastel pink.

"There's a reason why I like drop earrings," Lauri told me. She began revealing images of a childhood that changed her forever, a tale of truth and its power to transform.

It was a spring day. Lauri was in sixth grade, and her classroom was cheerfully decorated. Yellow May Day baskets hung suspended on clotheslines above desks, caged hamsters rustled in shredded newspaper and orange marigolds curled over cutoff milk cartons on window shelves.

The teacher, Mrs. Lake, stood in front of the class, her auburn hair flipping onto her shoulders like Jackie Kennedy's, her kind, blue eyes sparkling. But it was her drop earrings that Lauri noticed most— golden teardrop strands laced with ivory pearls. "Even from my back-row seat," Lauri recalled, "I could see those earrings gleaming in the sunlight from the windows."

Mrs. Lake reminded the class it was the day set aside for end-of-the-year conferences. Both parents and students would participate in these important progress reports. On the blackboard, an alphabetical schedule assigned 20 minutes for each family.

Lauri's name was at the end of the list. But it didn't matter much. Despite at least one reminder letter mailed home and the phone calls her teacher had made, Lauri knew her parents would not be coming.

Lauri's father was an alcoholic, and that year his drinking had escalated. Many nights Lauri would fall asleep hearing the loud, slurred voice of her father, her mother's sobs, slamming doors, pictures rattling on the wall.

The previous Christmas Lauri and her sister had saved baby-sitting money to buy their dad a shoeshine kit. They had wrapped the gift with red-and-green paper and trimmed it with a gold ribbon curled into a bow. When they gave it to him on Christmas Eve, Lauri watched in stunned silence as he threw it across the living room, breaking it into three pieces. Now Lauri watched all day long as each child was escorted to the door leading into the hallway, where parents would greet their sons or daughters with proud smiles, pats on the back and sometimes even hugs. The door would close, and Lauri would try to distract herself with her assignments. But she couldn't help hearing the muffled voices as parents asked questions, children giggled nervously and Mrs. Lake spoke. Lauri imagined how it might feel to have her parents greet her at the door.

When at last everyone else's name had been called,

Mrs. Lake opened the door and motioned for Lauri. Silently Lauri slipped out into the hallway and sat down on a folding chair. Across from the chair was a desk covered with student files and projects. Curiously she watched as Mrs. Lake looked through the files and smiled.

Embarrassed that her parents had not come, Lauri folded her hands and looked down at the linoleum. Moving her desk chair next to the downcast little girl, Mrs. Lake lifted Lauri's chin so she could make eye contact. "First of all," the teacher began, "I want you to know how much I love you."

Lauri lifted her eyes. In Mrs. Lake's face she saw things she'd rarely seen: compassion, empathy, tenderness.

"Second," the teacher continued, "you need to know it is not your fault that your parents are not here today."

Again Lauri looked into Mrs. Lake's face. No one had ever talked to her like this. No one.

"Third," she went on, "you deserve a conference whether or not your parents are here or not. You deserve to hear how well you are doing and how wonderful I think you are."

In the following minutes, Mrs. Lake held a conference just for Lauri. She showed Lauri her grades. She scanned Lauri's papers and projects, praising her efforts and affirming her strengths. She had even saved a stack of of watercolors Lauri had painted.

to my friend

Lauri didn't know exactly when, but at some point in that conference she heard the voice of hope in her heart. And somewhere a transformation started.

As tears welled in Lauri's eyes, Mrs. Lake's face became misty and hazy—except for her drop earrings of golden curls and ivory pearls. What were once irritating intruders in oyster shells had been transformed into things of beauty.

It was then that Lauri realized, for the first time in her life, that she was lovable.

As we sat together in a comfortable silence, I thought of all the times Lauri had worn the drop earrings of truth for me.

I, too, had grown up with an alcoholic father, and for years I had buried my childhood stories. But Lauri had met me in a symbolic hallway of empathy. There she helped me see that the shimmering jewel of self-worth is a gift from God that everyone deserves. She showed me that even adulthood is not too late to don the dazzling diamonds of new-found self-esteem.

Just then the kids ran up and flopped onto the grass to dramatize their hunger. For the rest of the afternoon we wiped spilled milk, praised off-balance somersaults and glided down slides much too small for us.

But in the midst of it all, Lauri handed me a small box, a birthday gift wrapped in a red floral paper trimmed with a gold bow.

I opened it. Inside was a pair of drop earrings.

—*Nancy Sullivan-Geng*

Footnote: Reprinted with permission of the Reader's Digest Association, Inc.

If we could read the secret history of our enemies, we would find in each man's life a sorrow and a suffering enough to disarm all hostility.

HENRY WADSWORTH LONGFELLOW

Men are born equal but they are also born different.

ERICH FROMM

Women lie about their age; men about their income.

WILLIAM FEATHER

Men are but children, too, though they have gray hairs; they are only of a larger size.

SENECA

Beautiful Things

The best and the most
beautiful things in life
cannot be seen or even touched...
they must be felt with the heart.

—Helen Keller

The Guest Book

When I was young, I'd visit folks
who lived on neighboring streets.
A widow often asked me in
for tea and pastry treats.

She made me feel special with
a table set just so,
while she would talk of baking and
how long to raise the dough.

Politely, I would listen although
thoughts would often stray.
Each time I left, I gave my word
I'd come another day.

Before I went to college
she asked that I stop by.
She opened up her old guest book
while trying not to cry.

Then as she paged through many years,
in pen I saw my name.
For she had written in that book
the days and times I came.

"You won't learn this in textbooks,"
she softly said to me—
"how you can lift another's soul
with just a cup of tea."

—Carla Muir
from Stories for the Heart

Valentines

L ittle Chad was a shy, quiet young fella. One day he came home and told his mother he'd like to make a valentine for everyone in his class. Her heart sank. She thought, *I wish he wouldn't do that!* because she had watched the children when they walked home from school. Her Chad was always behind them. They laughed and hung on to each other and talked to each other. But Chad was never included. Never-the-less, she decided she would go along with her son. So she purchased the paper and glue and crayons. For three whole weeks, night after night, Chad pains-takingly made thirty-five valentines.

Valentine's Day dawned, and Chad was beside himself with excitement! He carefully stacked them up, put them in a bag, and bolted out the door. His mom decided to bake him his favorite cookies and serve them up warm and nice with a cool glass of milk when he came home from school. She just knew he would be disappointed...maybe that would ease the pain a little. It hurt her to think that he wouldn't get many valentines—maybe none at all.

That afternoon she had the cookies and milk on the table. When she heard the children outside she looked out the window. Sure enough here they came, laughing and having the best time. And, as always, there was Chad in the rear. He walked a little faster than usual. She fully expected him to burst into tears as soon as he got inside. His arms were empty, she noticed, and when the door opened she choked back the tears.

"Mommy has some warm cookies and milk for you."

But he hardly heard her words. He just marched right on by, his face aglow, and all he could say was:

"Not a one...not a one."

And then he added, "I didn't forget a one, not a single one!"

—*Dale Galloway*
from Dream a New Dream

A Perfect Pot of Tea

An impatient crowd of nearly two hundred diehard bargain hunters shoved their way into the huge living room of the old Withers' homestead. The sweltering 90-degree temperature didn't deter a single one, all in pursuit of the estate sale find of the summer.

The lady conducting the sale, a long-time acquaintance, nodded as we watched the early morning scavengers. "How's this for bedlam?" she chuckled.

I smiled in agreement. "I shouldn't even be here. I have to be at the airport in less than an hour," I admitted to her. "But when I was a teenager, I sold cosmetics in this neighborhood. And Hillary Withers was my favorite customer."

"Then run and check out the attic," she suggested. "There are plenty of old cosmetics up there."

Quickly, I squeezed through the ever-growing throng and climbed the stairs to the third floor. The attic was deserted except for a petite elderly woman presiding over several tables loaded with yellowed bags of all sizes.

"What brings you all the way up here?" she asked as she popped the stopper out of a perfume bottle. "There's nothing up here except old Avon, Tupperware, and Fuller Brush products."

I drew in a long, cautious breath. The unmistakable fragrance of "Here's My Heart" perfume transported me back nearly 20 years.

"Why, this is my own handwriting!" I exclaimed as

my eyes fell upon an invoice stapled to one of the bags. The untouched sack held more than a hundred dollars' worth of creams and colognes. This had been my very first sale to Mrs. Withers.

On that long-ago June day, I'd canvassed the wide, tree-lined avenue for nearly four hours, but not one lady-of-the-house had invited me inside. As I rang the bell at the last house, I braced myself for the now-familiar rejection.

"Hello, Ma'am, I'm your new Avon representative," I stammered, when the carved-oak door swung open. "I have some great products I'd like to show you." When my eyes finally found the courage to face the lady in the doorway, I realized it was Mrs. Withers, the bubbly, matronly soprano in our church choir. I'd admired her lovely dresses and hats, dreaming that someday I'd wear stylish clothes, too. Just two months before, when I'd traveled to a distant city to have brain surgery, Mrs. Withers had showered me with the most beautiful cards.

"Why, Roberta, dear, come in, come in," Mrs. Withers' voice sang out. "I need a million and one things. I'm so glad you came to see me."

Gingerly, I eased myself onto the spotless white sofa and unzipped my tweed satchel filled with all the cosmetic samples five dollars could buy. When I handed Mrs. Withers a sales brochure, suddenly I felt like the most important girl in the world.

"Mrs. Withers, we have two types of creams, one for ruddy skin tones and another for sallow skin," I explained with newfound confidence. "And they're great for wrinkles, too."

"Oh good, good," she chirped.

"Which one would you like to try?" I asked, adjusting the wig hiding my stubbly surgery-scarred scalp.

"Oh, I'll surely need one of each," she answered. "And what do you have in the way of fragrances?"

"Here, try this one, Mrs. Withers. They recommend that you place it on the pulse point for the best effect," I instructed, pointing to her diamond-and-gold clad wrist.

"Why, Roberta, you're so knowledgeable about all of this. You must have studied for days. What an intelligent young woman you are!"

"You really think so, Mrs. Withers?"

"Oh, I know so. And just what do you plan to do with your earnings?"

"I'm saving for college to be a registered nurse," I replied, surprised at my own words. "But today, I'm thinking more of buying my mother a cardigan sweater for her birthday. She always goes with me for my medical treatments, and when we travel on the train, a sweater would be nice for her."

"Wonderful, Roberta, and so considerate. Now what do you have in the gift line?" she asked, requesting two of each item I recommended.

Her extravagant order totaled $117.42. Had she meant to order so much? I wondered. But she smiled back and said, "I'll be looking forward to receiving my delivery, Roberta. Did you say next Tuesday?"

I was preparing to leave when Mrs. Withers said, "You look absolutely famished. Would you like some tea before you go? At our house, we think of tea as 'liquid sunshine.'"

I nodded, then followed Mrs. Withers to her

pristine kitchen, filled with all manner of curiosities. I watched, spellbound, as she orchestrated a tea party—like I'd seen in the movies—just for me. She carefully filled the tea kettle with cold water, brought it to a "true" boil, then let the tea leaves steep for exactly five long minutes. "So the flavor will blossom," she explained.

Then she arranged a silver tray with a delicate china tea set, a chintz tea cozy, tempting strawberry scones, and other small splendors. At home, we some-times drank iced tea in jelly glasses, but never had I felt like a princess invited to afternoon tea.

"Excuse me, Mrs. Withers, but isn't there a faster way to fix tea?" I asked. "At home, we use tea bags."

Mrs. Withers wrapped her arm around my shoulder. "There are some things in life that shouldn't be hurried," she confided. "I've learned that brewing a proper pot of tea is a lot like living a proper life. It takes extra effort, but it's always worth it.

"Take you, for instance, with all of your health problems. Why, you're steeped with determination and ambition, just like a perfect pot of tea. Many peo-ple in your shoes would give up, but not you. You can accomplish anything you set your mind to, Roberta."

Abruptly, my journey back in time ended when the lady in the hot, sticky attic asked, "You knew Hillary Withers, too?"

I wiped a stream of perspiration from my forehead. "Yes… I once sold her some of these cosmetics. But I can't understand why she never used them or gave them away."

"She did give a lot of them away," the lady replied

matter-of-factly. "But somehow, some of them got missed and ended up here."

"But why did she buy them and not use them?" I asked.

"Oh, she purchased a special brand of cosmetics for her own use." The lady spoke in a confidential whisper. "Hillary had a soft spot in her heart for door-to-door salespeople. She never turned any of them away. She used to tell me, 'I could just give them money, but money alone doesn't buy self-respect. So I give them a little of my money, lend a listening ear, and share my love and prayers. You never know how far a little encouragement can take someone.'"

I paused, remembering how my cosmetic sales had soared after I'd first visited Mrs. Withers. I bought my mother the new sweater from my commission on the sale, and I still had enough money for my college fund. I even went on to win several district and national cosmetics-sales awards. Eventually, I put myself through college with my own earnings and realized my dream of becoming a registered nurse. Later, I earned a master's degree and a Ph.D.

"Mrs. Withers really cared for all of these people?" I asked, pointing to the dozens of time-worn delivery bags on the table.

"Oh, yes," she assured me. "She did it without the slightest desire that anyone would ever know."

I paid the cashier for my purchases—the sack of cosmetics I'd sold to Mrs. Withers, and a tiny, heart-shaped gold locket. I threaded the locket onto the gold chain I wore around my neck. Then I headed for the airport; later that afternoon I was addressing a medical convention in New York.

When I arrived in the elegant hotel ballroom, I found my way to the speaker's podium and scanned the sea of faces—health-care specialists from all over the country. Suddenly, I felt as insecure as on that long-ago day, peddling cosmetics in that unfamiliar, affluent neighborhood.

Can I do it? my mind questioned.

My trembling fingers reached upward to the locket. It opened, revealing a picture of Mrs. Withers inside. I again heard her soft but emphatic words: "You can accomplish anything you set your mind to, Roberta."

"Good afternoon," I began slowly. "Thank you for inviting me to speak about putting the care back in health care. It's often said that nursing is love made visible. But this morning I learned an unexpected lesson about the power of quiet love expressed in secret. The kind of love expressed not for show, but for the good it can do in the lives of others. Some of our most important acts of love often go unnoticed. Until they've had some time to steep—for their flavor to blossom."

Then I told my colleagues the story of Hillary Withers. Much to my surprise, there was thunderous applause. And to think, it all began with a perfect pot of tea!

—*Roberta Messner*
from Country Victorian

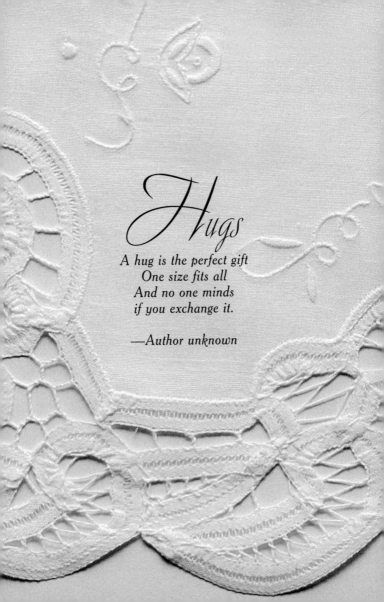

Hugs

A hug is the perfect gift
One size fits all
And no one minds
if you exchange it.

—Author unknown

The Story of the Praying Hands

About 1490 two young friends, Albrecht Dürer and Franz Knigstein, were struggling young artists. Since both were poor, they worked to support themselves while they studied art.

Work took so much of their time and advancement was slow. Finally, they reached an agreement: they would draw lots, and one of them would work to support both of them while the other would study art. Albrecht won and began to study, while Franz worked at hard labor to support them. They agreed that when Albrecht was successful he would support Franz who would then study art.

Albrecht went off to the cities of Europe to study. As the world now knows, he had not only talent but genius. When he had attained success, he went back to keep his bargain with Franz. But Albrecht soon discovered the enormous price his friend had paid. For as Franz worked at hard manual labor to support his friend, his fingers had become stiff and twisted. His slender, sensitive hands had been ruined for life. He could no longer execute the delicate brush strokes necessary to fine painting. Though his artistic dreams could never be realized, he was not embittered but rather rejoiced in his friend's success.

One day Dürer came upon his friend unexpectedly and found him kneeling with his gnarled hands intertwined in prayer, quietly praying for the success of his friend although he himself could no longer be an artist. Albrecht Dürer, the great genius, hurriedly sketched the folded hands of his faithful friend and later completed a truly great masterpiece known as "The Praying Hands."

Today art galleries everywhere feature Albrecht Dürer's works, and this particular masterpiece tells an eloquent story of love, sacrifice, labor and gratitude. It has reminded multitudes world around of how they may also find comfort, courage and strength.

—*Author unknown*

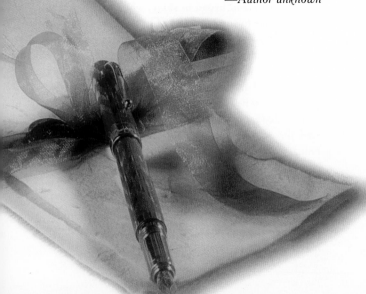

The Gift That Kept on Giving

I *was searching through Grandma's old trunk for some pictures when I came across a small, leather-bound book, the edges crumbly and dusty. It was a copy of* Snowbound, *and "John Greenleaf Whittier" was inscribed on the first page.*

"Look, Grandma," I said. "Is this the book you told me about that [your friend] Sarah Jane signed?"

"No," Grandma replied. She turned the book over lovingly. "This is the original one."

"But you sold that one to Warren Carter."

"I did," Grandma nodded. "The money he gave me helped get a coat with a fur collar for Ma's Christmas."

"But, how—?"

"How does it happen to be here? That's quite a story," Grandma said. "I guess I've never told you more than the first part of it."

"Tell me now," I urged her, and together we went back in time to my Grandma's high school years.

Warren Carter did give me five dollars for my autographed copy of Snowbound, and for four years I was content with the copy that Sarah Jane had signed to look like the original. Ma enjoyed her coat so much that I never regretted the choice I had made.

Just before we graduated from high school, Warren stopped in to see me one evening.

"Mabel," he said, "you've given me a run for my money ever since we started school together. I probably never would have studied so hard if you had been easier to beat. I think you deserve a graduation gift for making me work."

He handed me a wrapped and ribboned package, and grinned happily as I opened it. It was the copy of *Snowbound* I had sold to him in the eighth grade. "Oh, Warren! Are you sure you want me to have this back?"

He nodded. "It's too valuable a thing for you ever to have sold. You've been a good friend over the years, and I want you to keep it."

The book went with me to my new home, and whenever I looked at it I thought of Warren's generosity. Then one Christmas, when Alma was about eight years old, there was no money for gifts for the family. Sarah Jane and I made doll clothes from scraps for our daughters' dolls.

"What are you doing for Len this year?" Sarah Jane asked as we worked on our sewing. "You haven't said anything about it."

"I've made him a sweater and socks," I said, "but the truth is, I want to get him a Bible. We have a nice family Bible, and the church Bible, of course, but he needs a reading Bible the size of his hymnal. I could get one from the catalog for seventy-five cents, but it's bound in cloth. The one I really have my eye on is bound in French Morocco and has gold edges."

"How much is it?"

"$1.40. I pick it up and look at it every time I go into Gages' store. Maybe I'll give it so much wear that they'll lower the price."

"Dorcas would let you get it and pay a little at a time," Sarah Jane said. "In fact, she would insist, if she knew you wanted it."

I shook my head. "Len wouldn't enjoy reading it if he knew I'd gone into debt for it. He would say that a Bible here and one at the church is enough. But I know how much he'd like one he could carry with him."

"How much do you still need?"

"Seventy-five cents."

"More than you'll get for your eggs," Sarah Jane said. "What else could you sell?"

"Nothing that I know of." I shrugged. I thought for a moment. "Well, maybe there is. My autographed copy of *Snowbound*."

Sarah Jane was appalled. "Oh, Mabel, no! I was thinking of something to eat, like cream or vegetables. That book is priceless!"

"So is Len," I replied. "I'll take it in to Dorcas and see if she'll buy it. Or at least trade it for the Bible."

Sarah Jane wasn't convinced that this was a good idea, but she said no more. The next time I went into town, I took the slender volume and explained my plan to Dorcas Gage.

"Are you sure, Mabel?" she protested. "This book is a treasure. Mr. Whittier is dead now, and there may not be many autographed copies of one of his most famous poems."

"I know. But how often do I read it? Len would read his Bible every day."

Dorcas was reluctant, but she took the book in return for the Bible, and I hurried home, more than pleased with my bargain.

When gifts were opened on Christmas morning, Len was delighted, as I knew he would be. As usual, we shared the day with Thomas and Sarah Jane. As we prepared to leave their home that evening, Sarah Jane handed me a small package.

"One more little gift," she said.

When I opened the present, I very nearly burst into tears. It was my autographed copy of *Snowbound*.

"Who knows what that book might buy next year?" Sarah Jane said with a grin. "I figured this was the best investment you could ever have."

But she was mistaken. Actually, the best investment of my life had been her friendship.

—*Arleta Richardson*
from Grandmother's Attic

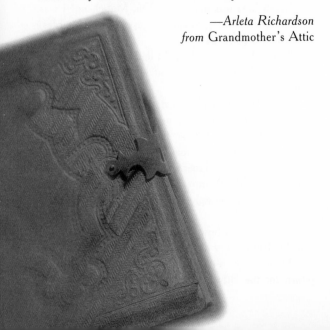

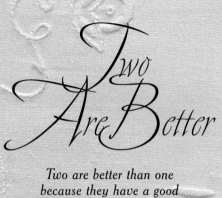

Two
Are Better

Two are better than one
because they have a good
return for their labor.
For if either of them falls,
the other will lift up his companion.
But woe to the one
who falls when there is not
one to lift him up.

—Ecclesiastes 4:9-10

In the Trenches

You've probably heard the powerful story coming out of World War I of the deep friendship of two soldiers in the trenches. Two buddies were serving together in the mud and misery of that wretched European stalemate (one version even identifies them as actual brothers). Month after month they lived out their lives in the trenches, in the cold and the mud, under fire and under orders.

From time to time one side or the other would rise up out of the trenches, fling their bodies against the opposing line and slink back to lick their wounds, bury their dead, and wait to do it all over again. In the process, friendships were forged in the misery. Two soldiers became particularly close. Day after day, night after night, terror after terror, they talked of life, of families, of hopes, of what they would do when (and if) they returned from this horror.

On one more fruitless charge, "Jim" fell, severely wounded. His friend, "Bill," made it back to the relative safety of the trenches. Meanwhile Jim lay suffering beneath the night flares. Between the trenches. Alone.

The shelling continued. The danger was at its peak. Between the trenches was no place to be. Still, Bill wished to reach his friend, to comfort him, to offer what encouragement only friends can offer. The officer in charge refused to let Bill leave the trench. It was simply too dangerous. As he turned his back, however, Bill went over the top. Ignoring the smell of cordite in the air, the concussion of incoming rounds, and the pounding in his chest, Bill made it to Jim.

Sometime later he managed to get Jim back to the safety of the trenches. Too late. His friend was gone. The somewhat self-righteous officer, seeing Jim's body, cynically asked Bill if it had been "worth the risk." Bill's response was without hesitation.

"Yes, sir, it was," he said. "My friend's last words made it more than worth it. He looked up at me and said, 'I knew you'd come.'"

—*Stu Weber*
from Locking Arms

Together

A man was walking in a wilderness. He became lost and was unable to find his way out. Another man met him. "Sir, I am lost, can you show me the way out of this wilderness?" "No," said the stranger, "I cannot show you the way out of the wilderness, but maybe if I walk with you, we can find it together."

— *Emery Nester*
from Depression

OTHER BOOKS COMPILED BY ALICE GRAY

Stories for the Heart
More Stories for the Heart
Christmas Stories for the Heart
Stories for the Family's Heart
Keepsakes for the Heart - Mother

KEEPSAKES FOR THE HEART—FRIENDSHIP
published by Multnomah Publishers, Inc.

© 1998 by Multnomah Publishers, Inc.
International Standard Book Number: 1-57673-383-1

All photographs © by David Bailey, except page 10 © by Claudia Kunin.
Book Design by Kevin Keller.
Printed in China

Unless otherwise indicated, Scripture quotations are from the
New American Standard Bible (NASB) © 1960, 1977 by the
Lockman Foundation

Multnomah is a trademark of Multnomah Publishers, Inc., and is
registered in the U.S. Patent and Trademark Office.

Every effort has been made to provide proper and accurate source
attribution for selections in this volume. Should any attribution be found
to be incorrect, the publisher welcomes written documentation supporting
correction for subsequent printings. For material not in the public domain,
selections were made according to generally accepted fair-use standards
and practices. The publisher gratefully acknowledges the cooperation of
publishers and individuals granting permission for use of longer selections;
please see the bibliography for full attribution of these sources.

For information:
MULTNOMAH PUBLISHERS, INC.
POST OFFICE BOX 1720
SISTERS, OREGON 97759

98 99 00 01 02 03—7 6 5 4 3 2

ACKNOWLEDGMENTS

Grateful acknowledgment is given to all who have contributed to this book. Any inadvertent omissions of credit will be gladly corrected in future editions.

"The Crazy Quilt" by Melody Carlson from *Patchwork of Love* (Sisters, Ore.: Multnomah Publishers, Inc., 1997). Used by permission.

"Chance Meeting" by Jane Kirkpatrick from *A Burden Shared* (Sisters, Ore.: Multnomah Publishers, Inc., 1998). Used by permission.

"Summer and Winter" by Pamela Reeve from *Relationships* (Sisters, Ore.: Multnomah Publishers, Inc., 1997). Used by permission.

"At the Winter Feeder" by John Leax from *The Task of Adam* (Grand Rapids, Mich.: Zondervan Publishing House, 1985). Used by permission of the author.

"Beethoven's Gift" by Philip Yancey from *Helping the Hurting* (Sisters, Ore.: Multnomah Publishers, Inc., 1984). Used by permission.

"Teardrops of Hope" by Nancy Sullivan Geng from *Reader's Digest*, September 1997. Used by permission of the author.

"The Guest Book" by Carla Muir © 1997. Used by permission of the author. Contact through Yates and Yates Communication Services, 714-285-8540.

"Valentines" by Dale Galloway © 1985. Used by permission of Scott Publishing.

"A Perfect Pot of Tea" by Roberta Messner, reprinted from *Country Victorian*, Fall 1996. Used by permission of the author.

"The Gift That Kept on Giving" by Arleta Richardson from *Christmas Stories from Grandma's Attic* (Colorado Springs, Colo.: Chariot/Victor Publishing, 1991). Used by permission.

"In the Trenches" by Stu Weber from *Locking Arms* (Sisters, Ore.: Multnomah Publishers, Inc., 1995). Used by permission.

"Together" by Emery Nester from *Depression* (Sisters, Ore.: Multnomah Publishers, Inc., 1983).